NORTH EASTERN PACIFICS—a pictorial survey

NORTH EASTERN
PACIFICS

---

a pictorial survey

NORMAN E. PREEDY

D. BRADFORD BARTON LIMITED

Frontispiece: Peppercorn Class A1 No. 60162 *St. Johnstoun*, the last member of the class to be built, drifts through Princes Street Gardens, heading towards Edinburgh (Waverley) to take over a southbound train.

© *copyright D. Bradford Barton Ltd 1974*

printed in Great Britain by Chapel River Press (IPC Printers), Andover, Hants.

for the publishers

D. BRADFORD BARTON LTD · Trethellan House · Truro · Cornwall · England

Class A4 4-6-2 No.60009 Union of South Africa, as preserved by the Lochty Private Railway Company near Anstruther in Fifeshire. Scotland.

introduction

The London & North Eastern Railway was blessed with a good proportion of Pacific locomotives with which to work its express passenger services and from December 1949, when the last of this type was turned out from Doncaster Works, until 1958, its stud numbered no less than 202. After 1959, when the first diesels came onto the scene in growing numbers, the Pacifics were withdrawn, slowly at first but in increasing numbers until 1966, when the last of them was retired.

The actual make up of the 202 Pacifics was 34 Class A4, 78 Class A3, 40 Class A2, and 50 Class A1. Perhaps the best known and most loved of these were the handsome streamlined A4s designed by Nigel Gresley. The first was turned out at Doncaster Works—nicknamed 'The Plant'—in September 1935 and the order completed in 1938.

The LNER and its successors, the Eastern, North Eastern and Scottish Regions of British Railways, was publicity minded and this was shown in the number of named services operated. Such famous trains as 'The Elizabethan', 'The Heart of Midlothian', 'The Tees-Tyne Pullman' and, best known of all, 'The Flying Scotsman', come to mind. On all these the Pacifics were standard power.

The names bestowed on these locomotives were an interesting feature and some became household words. One batch, based on a selection of wild birds, included the famous A4 No.60022 *Mallard*, celebrated as the holder of the blue riband of speed with steam—by virtue of its 126mph run in June 1938. Other names carried by the Pacifics included those of countries within the Commonwealth, plus names of LNER officials and Chief Mechanical Engineers. The A2 and A3 classes were mostly named after famous race horses and carried such unusual names as *Blink Bonny*—winner of the Oaks and Derby in 1857—and *Robert the Devil* after the winner of the St. Leger in the year 1880. The more modern Class A1, designed by A. H. Peppercorn and built at both Doncaster and Darlington workshops, was first introduced in 1948, the last one being completed in December 1949. These carried a mixture of names in the same vein as the previous types, although one batch was romantically christened after characters in Sir Walter Scott's novels including *Hal o' the Wynd*, *Madge Wildfire* and *Redgauntlet*. An interesting variation occurred in that some of the A1s were named after the constituent companies which had gone to make up the LNER: *Great Northern*, No. 60113—not a true A1 but a rebuild from the old Gresley Class A10; *North Eastern*, No. 60147; *Great Central*, No. 60156; *Great Eastern*, No. 60157 and *North British*, No. 60161.

The Pacifics were spread throughout the main East Coast running sheds—Kings Cross, New England, Grantham, Doncaster, Copley Hill (Leeds), York, Gateshead, and Heaton (Newcastle). Over the Border they were also allocated to Haymarket and St. Margarets (Edinburgh), Dundee, and Ferryhill (Aberdeen), whilst Carlisle (Canal) depot had a small stud for working over the Waverley route. Most of the time, the top-link power was kept in immaculate condition, both internally and externally. Some sheds, notably Kings Cross and Haymarket, had particularly good reputations for turning out very smart locomotives, and some of their A4s had to be seen to be believed.

It is a happy thought that several of these magnificent Pacifics are preserved in Britain, the United States (A4 No. 60008 *Dwight D. Eisenhower*) and Canada (A4 No. 60010 *Dominion of Canada*). No less than three A4s are preserved in this country in working order, whilst a fourth member of the class, *Mallard*, is in the National Collection to be exhibited in the new Railway Museum at York. In addition, the A3 and A2 classes are represented in preservation by the famous *Flying Scotsman* and *Blue Peter*. Thus something of what was once the glory of the old LNER is still with us in these days of modern diesel and electric locomotives.

Class A4 4-6-2 No. 60004 *William Whitelaw* at Darlington on a Railway Correspondence & Travel Society Railtour.

Class A4

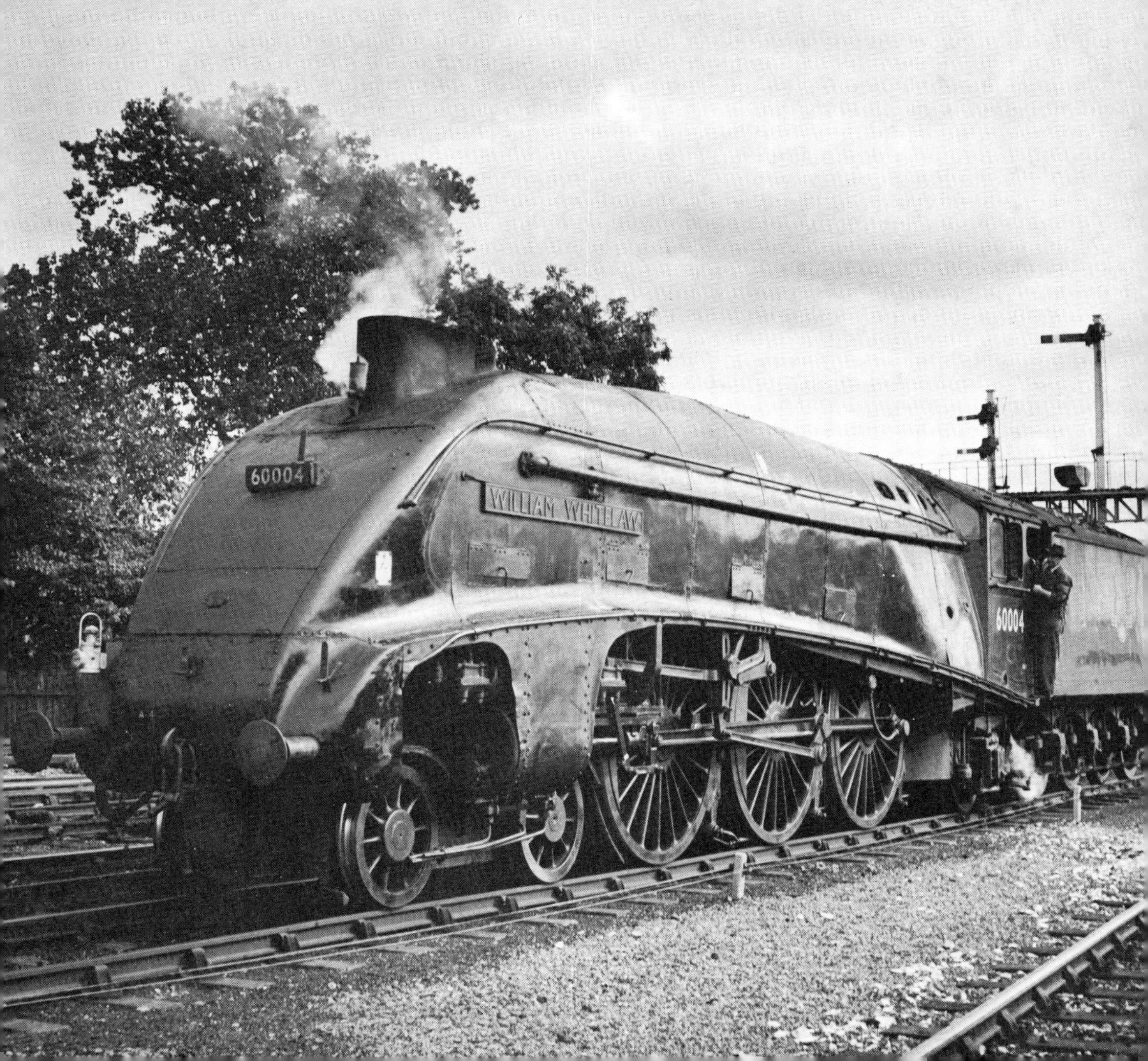

Class A4 No. 60009 *Union of South Africa* at Newcastle Central with 'The Talisman' from Kings Cross to Edinburgh. It is interesting to note the plaque on the cab side which bears the coat of arms of the Union of South Africa. This was replaced, on the nearside cab, by a rectangular steel plate depicting a springbok.

Class A4 No. 60024 *Kingfisher* on foreign metals at Hamworthy Junction on the Southern Region, having been brought down from Scotland for a weekend of railtours in the south. This view dates from 26 March 1966, when *Kingfisher* worked a tour—organised by the 'A4 Preservation Society'—which took the Pacific through to Weymouth.

No. 60024 *Kingfisher* again, leaving Stirling with the 1.30 p.m. Aberdeen–Glasgow (Buchanan Street) train (above) on 31 August 1965 when this service was the regular preserve of an A4. Below: also at Stirling, No. 60024 displays a 61B (Aberdeen Ferryhill) shed plate. The A4s ended their days in Scotland working between Glasgow and Aberdeen. From 1954 a small plaque depicting a kingfisher was carried on the diamond-shaped plate affixed to the boiler.

Class A 4 No. 60016 *Silver King*, in a very run-down condition and in need of a visit to Doncaster Works, is working out the mileage as she leaves Askham Tunnel, between Tuxford and Retford, with a down goods on 8 August 1956.

Class A 4 No. 60028 *Walter K. Whigham* records an 'on time' arrival at Kings Cross at 4.20 p.m. with the non-stop 'Elizabethan' from Edinburgh. This express had an average of 60mph start-to-stop over the 392·9 mile run.

Class A 4 No. 60029 *Woodcock* speeds through Welwyn Garden City on the main line with a down express for Newcastle.

The up Tees-Tyne Pullman, headed by an immaculate Kings Cross A4, No.60034 *Lord Faringdon*, about to cross the Scarborough lines into York, *en route* from Newcastle.

The northbound 'Elizabethan', introduced to commemorate the Coronation in 1953, passing Doncaster behind A4 No.60027 *Merlin*, from Haymarket shed. A crest depicting the badge of *HMS Merlin*, an Admiralty shore establishment, can be seen on the boiler casing.

One of the regular A4s on the Aberdeen–Glasgow service, No. 60024 *Kingfisher*, pauses at Perth in August 1965. Upon dieselisation on the East Coast main line, the remaining A4s were transferred to Scotland for working these services.

Class A4 No. 60006 *Sir Ralph Wedgwood* at Newcastle Central. The name, originally carried by LNER No. 4469, destroyed during an enemy air raid on York in 1942, was transferred in January 1944 to this locomotive, previously No. 4466 *Gadwall*.

Class A4 No. 60010 *Dominion of Canada* passing Retford with a train from Leeds in 1952. Her bell, presented by the Canadian Pacific Railway Company in 1935, could be rung by means of a steam supply taken from the whistle.

Undergoing overhaul for preservation in Canada, No. 60010 *Dominion of Canada* at Crewe Works in February 1967. She is now displayed in the Canadian Historical Railroads Association Museum in Montreal.

Class A4 No. 60009 *Union of South Africa* at Chaloners Whin with another south-bound express also on 17 July 1955. It would be interesting to know the name on the reversed train headboard, no doubt attached to the engine for a return working.

Class A4 No. 60017 *Silver Fox* on the outskirts of Retford with a Newcastle–Kings Cross express on 23 August 1952. The fireman is getting his fire into shape whilst the driver takes a breath of fresh air. Note the silver fox emblem on the boiler casing.

Class A4 No. 60033 *Seagull* speeds by on the level near Chaloners Whin, south of York, working a morning Edinburgh–Kings Cross express on 17 July 1955.

A look down the double chimney of A4 No. 60019 *Bittern* at Perth whilst working the 'Last Public A4 Run' organised by the Scottish Region from Glasgow to Aberdeen and back on 3 September 1966.

One of the most photogenic locations on the ex-GN main line is at Hadley Wood in the outer-London suburbs. In this view from the north end of the platform No. 60010 *Dominion of Canada* is heading for Kings Cross with an up express in June 1961. The bell, seen on page 17, was removed during 1957.

Class A4 No. 60014 *Silver Link* passing through Newcastle Central to pick up the 'Anglo Scottish Car Carrier', forerunner of one of today's Motor-railers. No. 60014 was one of the first batch of five A4s to be withdrawn from Kings Cross shed on 29 December 1962, after completing some 1½ million miles in 27 years. This makes an interesting comparison with 'Deltic' Class 55 No. 9010 (one of the A4s' replacements) which had already run two million miles in the first 12 years of its life.

The late afternoon sun glints off freshly applied paintwork on Class A4 No. 60008 *Dwight D. Eisenhower* heading northward from London with the 'Yorkshire Pullman'. The setting is Brookmans Park in the outer suburbs of London.

The 1.30 p.m. Aberdeen–Glasgow again, leaving Stirling with Class A4 No. 60009 *Union of South Africa* in charge, 27 August 1965.

Portrait of an A4: No. 60019 *Bittern* shows off the sleek lines of the class in this broadside view on the turntable at Ferryhill depot, Aberdeen, on 3 September 1966. The A4s were 71ft in length, with a working weight of 163 tons with a non-corridor tender.

Class A4 No. 60026 *Miles Beevor* exerts some of its 35,455lb tractive effort as it fights for adhesion on slippery rails at St. Margarets shed in Edinburgh, 2 October 1965.

Class A4 No. 60027 *Merlin* arrives on shed at Haymarket after bringing in 'The Flying Scotsman' which at this time was allowed 6 hours 58 minutes from London Edinburgh, including a stop at Newcastle.

Class A4 No.60031 *Golden Plover* at Perth in August 1965. The yellow stripe painted across the cabside denoted prohibition from working under the LM overhead electric network because of limited clearance—unlikely with an A4!

A line-up of express motive power at Doncaster shed on 29 April 1962: BR Standard 'Britannia' Class Pacific No.70011 *Hotspur* keeps company with A4 No.60021 *Wild Swan* and Gresley A3 No.60109 *Hermit*.

Class A4 No.60019 *Bittern* in a night scene at Leeds City after arrival with a rail tour on 25 November 1967.

Strange partners at Eastleigh on the Southern Region, 26 March 1966; No. 60024 *Kingfisher* and Bullied unrebui
West Country Class 4-6-2 No. 34006 *Bude.*

A portrait of A4 No. 60011 *Empire of India* outside Ferryhill shed at Aberdeen with preparations under way to get h
ready for the road. No. 60011 is fitted with one of the corridor tenders which were paired to many of the A4s
dispense with the need to stop for crew changes when working the non-stop expresses between Edinburgh a
London.

'Monarch of all he surveys' seems to be the pose adopted by Driver Day of Aberdeen as he looks down from the cab of Class A4 No. 60034 *Lord Faringdon*.

A close-up of the name-plate of one of the best known of all the A4s, No. 4498 *Sir Nigel Gresley* (ex-No. 60007) as preserved.

Driver Goldie at St. Rollox shed, Glasgow, gets A4 No. 60034 *Lord Faringdon* ready for the 17.30 from Buchanan Street to Aberdeen in September 1965.

The commemorative plaque fitted to A4 No. 60022 *Mallard*, holder of the world speed record for steam.

A4 No.60007 *Sir Nigel Gresley* undergoing overhaul in the erecting shop at Crewe Works ready for preservation, 1966. One could speculate for ever on the chalked inscription 'send for brown pork'!

Class A3

Sir Nigel Gresley's other Pacific design was the famous A3; No. 60085 *Manna*, fitted with double chimney, leaves West Hartlepool with a coast line train for Newcastle.

Class A3 No. 60039 *Sandwich*, in original condition with single chimney, clatters over the level crossing at East Markham, between Tuxford and Retford, with a Kings Cross–Newcastle express.

Class A3 No. 60057 *Ormonde* threads Princes Street Gardens at Edinburgh with a semi-fast from Aberdeen. She was turned out from Doncaster in February 1925 and withdrawn in October 1963.

Class A3 No. 60088 *Book Law*, paired with a GN pattern coal-railed tender, speeds downgrade from Askham Tunnel on 7 July 1956.

Class A3 No.60105 *Victor Wild* speeding southwards through Welwyn Garden City. She is fitted with smoke deflectors, similar to those on the German Federal Railways, which were introduced on this class from 1961 after successful experiments had been concluded.

A rather daunting name was carried by A3 No. 60110, *Robert the Devil*, named after the winner of the St. Leger in the year 1880. This photograph was taken at Doncaster with No. 60110 waiting to leave with an up express.

Overleaf: A portrait of one of Darlington's well-kept A3s, No. 60045 *Lemberg*, in the evening of her career. She was one of the class allocated to 'Bank Top' depot for main line standby duties in the early days of the diesels and many was the time she was called upon to take over from an ailing English Electric Class 40.

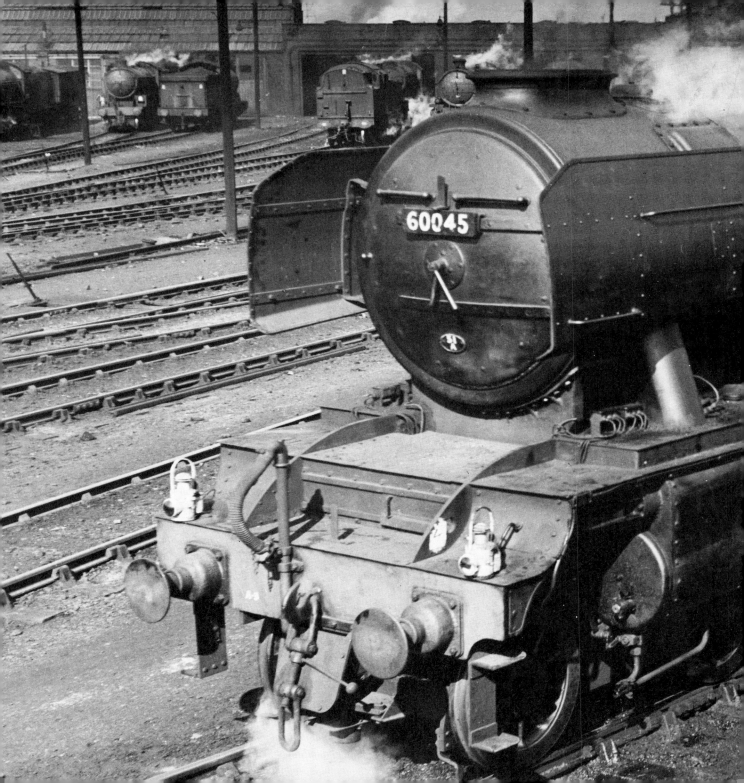

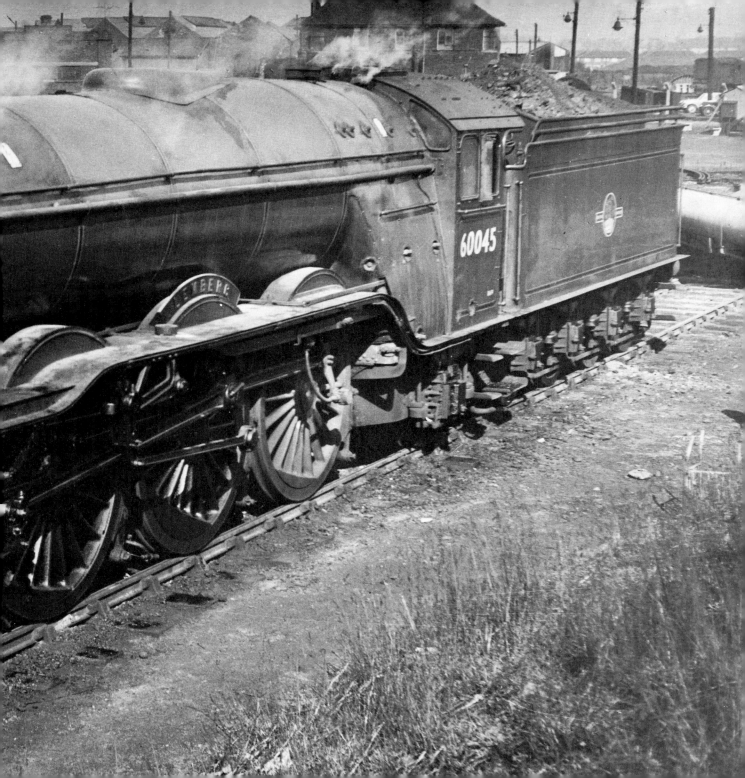

Class A3 No. 60038 *Firdaussi*, then based at Holbeck shed (Leeds), seen with an eleven coach Newcastle–Leeds train via the coast, June 1961.

supreme effort by A3 No. 60073 *St. Gatien* as she gets a heavy Kings Cross to Newcastle train (via the ⌐ast) under way after a stop on the tight curve at West Hartlepool.

Based at various depots in Scotland throughout its life A3 No. 60100 *Spearmint* is seen here in the yards at Hartlepools awaiting its train, a fitted northbound goods. She is paired with the LNER straight-sided style of tender.

The only Class A3 to carry the straight-sided smoke deflectors was No. 60097 *Humourist*, the subject of many experiments to improve smoke clearance. This Haymarket locomotive is seen here emerging from The Mound Tunnel into Waverley Station, Edinburgh, with a stopping train from Glasgow in May 1956.

A3 No. 60083 *Sir Hugo* and A4 No. 60017 *Silver Fox* at Kings Cross after arriving 'coupled light' from the Top Shed to work evening expresses. *Sir Hugo*, a comparative stranger to London, was one of a small number of northern-based A3s which retain a building plate on the centre splasher.

Grantham-based A3 No. 60064 *Tagalie* is coupled on to a Kings Cross express at Newcastle Central.
She will work the train as far as Grantham, being replaced there by another Pacific for the remaining
105 miles to London. *Tagalie* is fitted with a double chimney and has an L N E R straight-sided tender.

Class A3 No. 60086 *Gainsborough* pulls away from the stop at West Hartlepool with
Newcastle to Leeds train.

Class A3 No. 60070 *Gladiateur* at rest at Gateshead shed, 1959.

No. 60066, *Merry Hampton*, fresh from overhaul and in the final Class A3 condition, shows her paces near Potters Bar with a passenger 'running-in' turn from Kings Cross. The cab, with its uniquely high ventilator—clearly seen in this photograph—once belonged to sister A3 *St. Simon*.

The business end of No. 60051, *Blink Bonny*, waiting 'right away' from Newcastle with the 11 a.m. Glasgow (Queen Street) to Kings Cross 'Queen of Scots Pullman'. This particular A3 was often to be found on the most onerous passenger duties and the reversed headboard on the buffer beam indicates that she had recently worked another East Coast named express. The nameplate has Gill Sans lettering, unlike those on all the other A3s built before 1934.

Class A3 No. 60037 *Hyperion* heads light engine through Carlisle for the ex-NB shed at Canal after arriving with the southbound 'Waverley' express from Edinburgh, over the Waverley route. Engines were changed at Carlisle before 'The Waverley' continued its journey to London (St. Pancras) via Leeds.

Class A3 No. 60077 *The White Knight*, another member of the Holbeck Depot allocation, gets away from West Hartlepool with a Newcastle to Leeds train.

Class A3 No. 60096 *Papyrus* at Dundee in July 1958. This was the locomotive used in high speed trials during March 1935, running non-stop to Newcastle from London. On one trip Stoke summit was topped at 73mph and Newcastle (268 miles) reached in 230 minutes net. On the return journey *Papyrus* reached a speed of 108mph at Essendine with Driver Bill Sparshatt in charge.

Class A3 No. 60051 *Blink Bonny* arriving at Edinburgh (Waverley) from Haymarket shed to take over a south-bound working.

Immaculate Class A3 No. 60047 *Donovan* outside the depot at Grantham ready for a turn of duty. Grantham was important on the ex-GN main line as many trains stopped there to change either crews or locomotives.

Class A3 No. 60065 *Knight of Thistle* at New England depot (Peterborough) in May 1963. At this time steam was banned south of Peterborough on the main line and many Pacifics were transferred to here from Kings Cross when the latter depot closed.

Sporting a round-topped steam dome as opposed to the normal 'banjo' type is A3 No.60091 *Captain Cuttle* at St. Margaret's depot, Edinburgh.

anding on the coal stage road at Haymarket depot after the day's work is Class A3
b.60099 *Call Boy*, fitted with German-type smoke deflectors. No.60099 was based at
aymarket for over thirty years.

Alongside at Kings Cross, on Leeds and Newcastle trains, Class A3 No.60036 *Colombo*
and Class A4 No.60034 *Lord Faringdon*.

Class A3 No. 60063 *Isinglass* ready to leave Kings Cross with a northbound express in 1961. The works plate on the cabside reads 'London & North Eastern Railway No. 1618 Doncaster 1925'.

he best known of all the A3s is No. 4472 (ex-BR No. 60103) *Flying Scotsman*, bought for preservation A. F. Pegler in 1963. This locomotive has had a chequered career since then on railfan excursions this country as well as in the USA and Canada. Above, No. 4472 is seen at Cheadle Heath after an CGB railtour from London on 18 September 1965 and (below) in 1973, after its homecoming from the nited States and an ownership change to become the property of W. H. McAlpine, arriving at Didcot ith another LCGB railtour from Birmingham on 27 October.

Nameplates of two
Class A3s, No. 60046
Diamond Jubilee
and No. 60071 *Tranquil.*

Peppercorn Class A2
No. 60528 *Tudor
Minstrel* at the head
of an ARES railtour
at Manchester
(Exchange) on 23 Apr
1966. She had been
brought down from
Aberdeen for the
occasion.

Class A2

Class A2 No. 60532 *Blue Peter* standing at Perth with an Aberdeen to Glasgow train in the summer of 1966. In this view the double blastpipe and the rodding to the multiple valve regulator in the smoke box are clearly seen.

The mighty bulk of Class A2/2 No. 60504 *Mons Meg* lifts a heavy Glasgow–Kings Cross train around the curve at Chaloners Whin Junction, south of York. The six locomotives in Class A2/2 were Thompson rebuilds of the Gresley Class P 2-8-2s, originally designed for use between Edinburgh and Aberdeen.

Class A2/3 No. 60522 *Straight Deal* leaves Askham Tunnel with a down express. This locomotive, completed at Doncaster in June 1947, was among the last of the A2/3s to be withdrawn, after a life of exactly eighteen years.

Class A2/3 No.60517 *Ocean Swell* on shed in 1960 at Heaton depot (Newcastle). Note the tender construction with the use of 'snap headed' rivets.

Another Class A 2/3, No. 60516 *Hycilla*, also at Heaton shed. This locomotive was condemned in November 1962 after running 833,000 miles and at the time of the photograph still carried the earlier, rather ugly, pattern of chimney.

Class A2 No. 60529 *Pearl Diver* on the turntable at Haymarket depot, Edinburgh. Note the electric lighting fitted to this class, the generator being visible behind the nearside smoke shield.

The 6ft 2in driving wheels of the Class A2 Pacifics dominate this view of the motion of No. 60? *Sayajirao* at Dundee (Tay Bridge) shed, showing a wealth of detail for the railway modeller.

Class A2/3 No. 60521 *Watling Street* at Doncaster, 1959. The headlamps indicate use on a loose-coupled freight train.

Peppercorn Class A2 No. 60537 *Bachelors Button* at Ferryhill depot, Aberdeen. The long fire irons lying on the ground—now things of the past—must have been quite a job to handle on a rough-riding engine at speed.

A broadside view of Thompson Class A2/1 No.60509 *Waverley* at Eastfield shed in Glasgow. The storm sheet can be seen fitted across the gap between engine and tender. There were only four representatives of this sub-division of Class A2, built in 1944–45 in substitution for Gresley 'Green Arrow' 2-6-2s.

Thompson Class A2/1 No.60508 *Duke of Rothesay* at New England shed, Peterborough. The plain chimney fitted at the period this photograph was taken was later removed in favour of the standard type shown on No.60509.

Looking immaculate at the head of an express about to leave Aberdeen is Class A2 No. 60532 *Blue Peter*. This engine was allocated to Dundee depot from the summer of 1961, although here she wears a 61B plate. *Blue Peter* was withdrawn at the end of 1966, being stored at Dundee and Thornton Junction sheds. Later she was bought for preservation and taken to Doncaster Works for overhaul, being finished in LNER apple green livery and numbered 532 on the cab.

Class A2 No. 60530 *Sayajirao* at Dundee. Named after the Maharaja of Baroda's race-horse which won the St. Leger in 1947, she was one of three A2s to be transferred for a short while to the ex-Caledonian depot at Polmadie (Glasgow) in 1963.

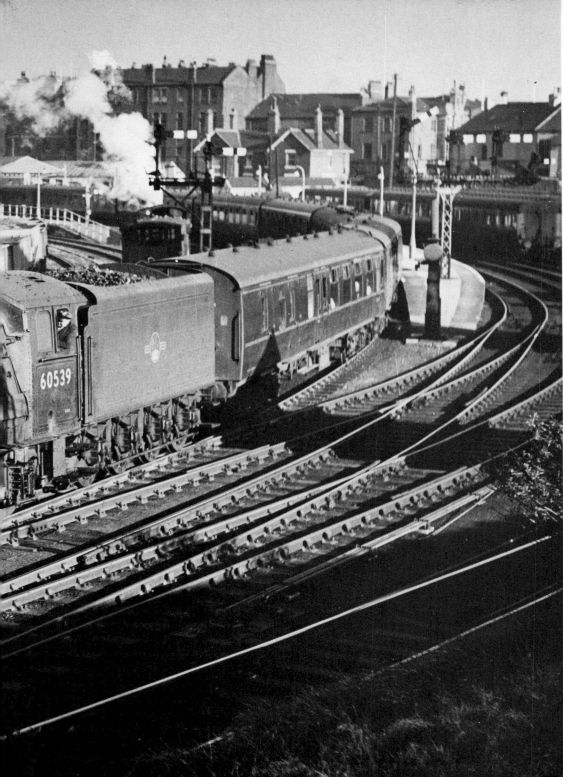

Peppercorn Class A2 No. 60539 *Bronzino* gets a heavy Newcastle bound train away from West Hartlepool on the last lap of its long journey from Kings Cross; 60539 was fitted with its double chimney when built, unlike some other members of the class, which were modified at later dates.

Class A1 Pacific No.60125 *Scottish Union* accelerates away from the Doncaster stop past Black Carr Junction with a Bradford to Kings Cross express on 28 June 1952. Note the tall LNER signals sited to clear the bridge over the main line.

The 49 engines in Peppercorn's Class A1 were built at Darlington and Doncaster in 1948/49. No.60161 *North British*, seen here arriving at Edinburgh Waverley, was one of the Doncaster-built batch.

Heading a heavy goods
from Millerhill yard at
Edinburgh, Class A1
No. 60131 *Osprey* gets
under way in August 1964
after a stop for water at
Hawick, on the 'Waverley'
line to Carlisle. The
smokebox carries a 55H shed
plate, signifying allocation
to Neville Hill depot at
Leeds.

Class A1 No. 60147 *North Eastern*, one of four in the class named after constituent companies of the LNER, on a Kings Cross–Newcastle train on the curve leaving West Hartlepool.

Beneath the footbridge leading to the works, Class A1 No. 60128 *Bongrace* waits to leave Doncaster for Kings Cross. This station was always worth a visit, with incessant activity and a very popular place for trainspotters.

Class A1 No. 60130 *Kestrel* arriving at Kings Cross with a train from Leeds and Bradford. The regulator is still open the express is lifted up the final short sharp gradient from Gasworks Tunnel. Note the sign calling attention to 8mph speed restriction into the tunnel.

Class A1 No. 60120 *Kittiwake*, at the head of the southbound 'Harrogate Sunday Pullman', passes Retford. These fine Pacifics were withdrawn after an extremely short life averaging only 15 years.

Another Class A1, No. 60144 *King's Courier*, heads up the main line away from Retford with the London bound 'Yorkshire Pullman'. This left Harrogate at 10.7 a.m., further coaches from Hull and Bradfor being attached at Doncaster.

Copley Hill-based A1 No. 60133 *Pommern* passes Tuxford Junction between Retford and Newark wi 'The Queen of Scots' Pullman. The lines crossing in the background carried the now disused Gre Central route from Chesterfield to Lincoln.

Five members of Class A1 were fitted with roller bearings, one of these being No. 60155 *Borderer*, seen here coasting into West Hartlepool from Newcastle with a train for Kings Cross.

No. 60150 *Willbrook* at Doncaster with a train for London, in 1960. During its career this Class A1 was allocated to three different depots, namely Heaton, Gateshead and York.

The last to be produced of the A1s was No. 60162 *St. Johnstoun*, based throughout on Edinburgh. She is here passing Newcastle at the head of a parcels train.

The first Peppercorn Class A1, No. 60114 *W. P. Allen*, was named at a ceremony in Kings Cross on 28 October 1948 in honour of a trade union member of the Railway Executive who had at one time been a driver.

Doncaster again, and quaintly named A1 No. 60135 *Madge Wildfire* about to leave for Kings Cross.

A Sunday morning at Doncaster shed in April 1962, with Class A1s No. 60119 *Patrick Stirling* facing No. 60144 *King's Courier*.

Class A1 4-6-2 No. 60152 *Holyrood* outside Gateshead shed during its reconstruction to a diesel-maintenance depot. Other locomotives in the picture are Class V2 2-6-2 No. 60970 and a Class J27 0-6-0.

Overleaf: Class A1 Pacific No. 60143 *Sir Walter Scott*, resplendent after a visit to Doncaster Works and the pride of Heaton shed, waits to leave Newcastle for Edinburgh.

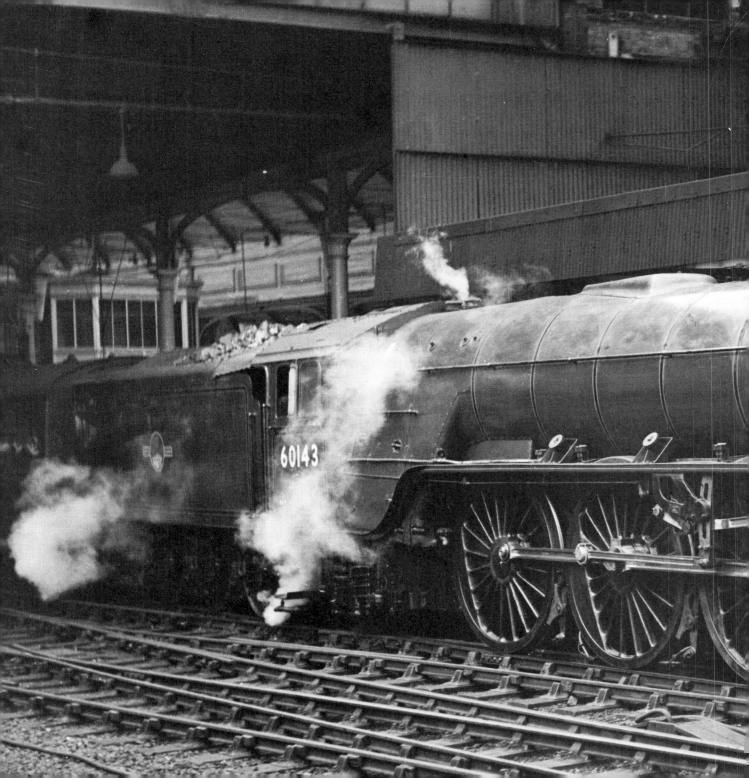

Inside the repair shop at York in July 1964 No. 60145 *Saint Mungo* receives attention. She was to be the last remaining member of the class and in 1965 was used on a WRS railtour in the Midlands from Birmingham (Moor Street) to Banbury. She was finally condemned in June of the following year, having been withdrawn in March and reinstated in April. No other Pacific was given a reprieve.

A Sunday morning visit to Gateshead shed could always be relied upon to produce some Pacifics at rest; in this scene are A1s No. 60159 *Bonnie Dundee* and a rather grimy No. 60147 *North Eastern*.

Following withdrawal of the Darlington standby A3s, ready for use in the event of a diesel failure, th
depot used A1s in this capacity and here No.60124 *Kenilworth* is seen on duty. This engine was th
penultimate member of the class to be withdrawn.

Darlington-built No.60154 *Bon Accord* displays the fine lines of the A1s.

A close-up of the nameplate of No. 60147 *North Eastern*. The finely detailed coats of arms on the A1s, named after constituent companies, were hand-painted.

The rather simpler nameplate of No. 60127, *Wilson Worsdell*. This A1 was named by the Mayor of Gateshead in a ceremony at Newcastle station in October 1950, after the CME of the North Eastern Railway from 1890 to 1910.

The 6ft 8in driving wheels of A1 Pacific No. 60124 *Kenilworth* make an impressive close-up at New England shed, Peterborough, in May 1963. Notice the 'Wakefield' mechanical lubricators on the running plate.

The remains of Class A3 Pacific No.60041 *Salmon Trout* (above) in the works yard at Cowlairs (Glasgow) in August 1966, the last but one of the A3s to be withdrawn. A chalk inscription on the buffer beam reads 'Thanks for the Memory'. A happier note is struck (below) by a Class A4, immaculate in LNER garter blue livery. Bearing its old number of 4498, *Sir Nigel Gresley* is seen during a BR Open Day at Neville Hill depot, Leeds, during March 1973.